I wish to express my sincere appreciation to my students: to Charles Peck for his unlimited advice and help in proofreading the entire manuscript; to Nelson Colon and Frank Camacho for posing in the photos to help make this book more expressive; and to Bernard MacSweeney for his excellent photographs.

Flying Roundhouse Kick by Master Sihak Henry Cho, with Mr. Julio LaSalle, former All American Champion

BETTER KARATE

for Boys

7/75

Sihak Henry Cho

DODD, MEAD & COMPANY · NEW YORK

Distributed in Canada by
McClelland and Stewart Limited, Toronto
Manufactured in the United States of America

8   9   10

Library of Congress Cataloging in Publication Data

Cho, Sihak Henry.
    Better karate for boys.

    Summary: Traces the history of karate, discusses the
philosophy of the sport, describes the various forms, and
gives directions for the major stances, punches, kicks,
and blocks.
    1. Karate—Juvenile literature. [1. Karate] I. Title.
GV1114.32.C49   1984   796.8'153   84–8089
ISBN 0–396–06568–6 (hard)
ISBN 0–396–08477–X (pbk.)

CONTENTS

WHAT IS KARATE?

Karate is the English equivalent of two Japanese characters meaning empty (kara) and hand (te). As nearly as can be determined, karate first began in India several thousand years ago. It was brought to China about 1500 years ago by the Indian Buddhist Monk, Daruma.

From China, karate was brought to Okinawa, where it was superimposed on the native Okinawan fighting technique and the resulting combination was called "Okinawate" or, literally, the Okinawa hand. From Okinawa, karate spread to other countries. Master Gichin Funakoshi was largely responsible for bringing Okinawate to Japan, which marked the beginning of modern Japanese karate. This was when karate was officially brought before the public, for in the past it had always been practiced secretly.

Karate, as mentioned previously, is a Japanese word. Different words are used in Chinese (Kung Fu) and Korean (Tae-Kwon Do) to designate the same or similar art. In the United States of America, the word "karate" is used as if it applies to the martial art of all Oriental countries. This is because the Americans first learned about it from the Japanese when United States soldiers were stationed there in the 1940's following the Second World War. The Korean karate art, tae kwon do, was not encountered by Americans until the Korean conflict in the 1950's. Also, Japanese instructors were the first to arrive in the United States and, later, the first books to be published in English were by Japanese. For these reasons, the term "karate" has been used generally and without reference to the Japanese martial art specifically.

The primary national forms of karate are Chinese, Japanese (including Okinawan), and Korean. The distinctive characteristics of the three styles can be seen through demonstrations and tournaments. The Japanese stylists favor simple movements, while the Koreans use many combined moves, particularly combinations of kicks. Chinese practitioners use flowing, circular movements as opposed to the sharp, linear movements of the Japanese and Koreans. It would seem that the Japanese spend more time applying their basic techniques to prearranged movements such as forms, while the Koreans are chiefly concerned with the application of basic moves to free fighting.

WHAT IS KUNG FU?

Kung fu presently means the Chinese style of karate. It originally covered all the Chinese martial arts. Kung fu has been practiced and developed by many different masters with different tastes and individualistic techniques, which accounts for its many different styles rather than the division into different arts of Tae-Kwon Do, Yudo, Hapkido, etc., in Korea, and Karate, Judo, Aikido, Jiu-Jitsu, etc., in Japan, on the basis of the distinct characteristics of each art.

Historically, the Chinese people practiced this art secretly, and this brought about not only the birth of its various styles but also the failure to unify the styles under set rules and regulations. Its techniques have never been open to the public, and it may not be considered as a popular sport but rather an individualistic self-defense form which should have been much more widespread than it is now.

Even if more than half of the kung fu techniques are primarily designed for the use of weapons such as sword, staff, spears, trident, steel chain, etc., the modern-day kung fu seems to be practiced with unarmed offensive and defensive moves. Generally, in kung fu training, the hands are kept open as opposed to the closed fist position used in tae-kwon do and karate. The combined moves in its form practices are performed slowly but smoothly and continuously. Most of a kung fu class is occupied with form practices and its students are supposed to spend many, many years to achieve internal power out of the forms. Free fighting is seldom seen in the class, but some prearranged fighting moves are occasionally practiced between advanced students.

WHAT IS TAE-KWON DO?

Tae-kwon do is Korean word for karate, recently agreed upon by the Korean Association. It is composed of three Korean characters which mean foot (tae), fist (kwon), and martial art (do). The word tae-kwon do replaced other Korean terms such as Tang-soo do, Kong-soo do, Tae-soo do, etc. Presently all tae-kwon do schools are unified under the Korean Tae-Kwon Do Association.

The forerunner of tae-kwon do was a system of Korean foot fighting called tae kyun which was developed over 1,000 years ago. Modern tae-kwon do derives from tae kyun, Chinese kung fu, and okinawate. Tae-kwon do is clearly related to Japanese karate, and for some time there has been an international competition between Japan and Korea. Tae-kwon do has gained much publicity recently because of its use in Vietnam by the Korean troops there. Presently, tae-kwon do schools are to be found throughout the world.

Tae-kwon do, as a modern karate form, provides the most scientific application of the basic movements to free fighting, which is the main goal of tae-kwon do. Special emphasis is placed on kicking techniques such as the popular hook kick which did not exist ten years ago. Usually, the trainees in a tae-kwon do class learn the basic moves, then apply them in prearranged movements and forms, and finally begin to apply them in free fighting. By train-

ing in the movements of tae-kwon do, the trainees can achieve physical fitness, ability at free fighting, and finally one of the strongest forms of self-defense known.

HOW TO WEAR AND FOLD
THE TRAINING UNIFORM

The training uniform is usually made of a tough cotton and is designed to allow the most freedom of movement. In Korean, this suit is called "do pok," *do* meaning "martial art" and *pok* meaning "suit."

The pants are put on first and tied at the front with the strings attached. The jacket is worn with the left flap over the right and tied at the right side.

The uniform, which is usually white in color, should always be kept clean by frequent washing. Patches, such as school insignia, worn on the uniform should be kept to a minimum.

When the uniform is folded to be carried, the pants and jacket are rolled up separately, then put together and tied with the belt.

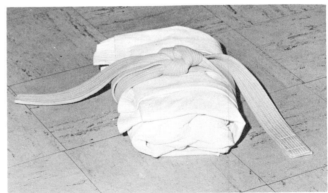

HOW TO TIE THE BELT

Hold the belt in front of you with both hands, the center of the belt facing the center of your waist. Wrap it around your waist so the belt crosses at the center of your back. Bring the two ends to the front of your waist. Adjust the length of the belt so that one end is slightly longer than the other. Cross the longer end over the shorter so that there are three strands of the belt at the center of your waist. Tuck the top strand under both the other strands and pull it through. Tighten the belt by pulling on the two ends. Tie a square knot by placing one end over the other, then tuck the top end under the second and, grasping both ends, pull the knot tight.

DEGREES AND BELT COLORS

There are basically two categories of tae-kwon do trainees—those in the under black belt category and those who hold a black belt. The under black belt ranks are called "kup," and each two kup are represented by a different belt color. The lowest kup is eighth and the highest first.

White belt—has no rank; beginner
Yellow belt—seventh and eighth kup; advanced beginner
Green belt—fifth and sixth kup   ⎫
Purple belt—third and fourth kup   ⎬ intermediate
Brown belt—first and second kup; advanced

The black belt ranks are called "dan," and the lowest rank is first dan. The first dan is considered a proficient student and he begins to learn the more advanced and complex techniques. He also begins to instruct, under supervision, lower-ranking students in basic movements. As he becomes better, he is promoted to higher ranks (second dan, and then third, and so forth) until he has mastered the movements and is considered a master or grand master.

First and second dan—assistant instructor
Third and fourth dan—instructor
Fifth and sixth dan—master
Seventh and higher—grand master

Black belts usually participate in national and international competitions up to the rank of fourth dan, although the team captain is sometimes a fifth dan. The ranks of the coaches are usually sixth dan and higher. In Japanese karate the tenth dan is the highest rank, while in Korea ninth dan is the highest, since ten is an unpopular number there.

THE TRAINING EQUIPMENT

Different pieces of equipment are used in tae-kwon do training. Some are intended to develop strength and coordination, others to improve speed and agility. The principal equipment used in a tae-kwon do gymnasium are shown in the photographs.

Left: PUNCHING BOARD Used for practicing punches and strikes. The purpose of this board is to aid in developing a strong hand.

Center: SPEED BAG This is the same as that used by boxers. It is intended to help the trainee develop timing and coordination. Usually punches and kicks are practiced on it.

Right: KICKING BALL Used to develop jumping ability and coordination for flying kicks.

Left Above: HEAVY BAG Another piece of equipment that is also used extensively by boxers. Practice on this will enable the trainee to increase the power of his attacks. It is used to practice both hand and kicking techniques.

Left: WEIGHTS Although these do not relate directly to martial arts training, the lifting of light weights will aid in developing overall bodily strength.

Above: MIRROR Practicing tae-kwon do techniques in front of a mirror enables you to observe yourself and correct any errors you may be making.

WHAT A CLASS CONSISTS OF

A tae-kwon do class begins when the instructor steps onto the floor and calls the students to attention. Usually an opening ritual is observed in which the students bow in unison to their instructor, who in return bows to them. The instructor is called in Korean Kyosah Nim and master instructor, Sahbum Nim. This mutual respect of student for teacher, teacher for student, and student for student, is part of the discipline and courtesy essential to the practice of the martial art.

Since physical conditioning is an important part of the practice of tae-kwon do, the class begins with calisthenics. Calisthenics are necessary for at least two reasons. First, they allow a student to gradually limber up his joints, tendons and muscles, thereby avoiding injury by too sudden movement. Secondly, they condition and strengthen him for the strenuous demands made by the practice of this martial art. Because of the time limitation, in-class calisthenics are usually limited to ten to fifteen minutes. Of course, the hard-working student will wish to devote considerably more time to body conditioning outside of class. No matter what rank a student holds, he must always maintain a high degree of physical fitness if he is to be successful in any martial art.

After the calisthenics are finished, the instructor usually has the students practice as a group the basic movements of tae-kwon do—the kicks, punches, blocks and stepping. The students often move up and down the floor in unison, performing at the signal of the instructor the particular movements he names. All levels of students participate, since the advanced students as well as the beginners must constantly practice these movements in order to build a strong foundation.

When the basic movements have been practiced long enough according to the judgment of the instructor, a break is given which lasts five to ten minutes. After the break, the class is often divided according to the levels of the students, with each group of students practicing what is appropriate to their level. For example, under the guidance of an instructor, the beginning white belts will continue to practice the basic movements. The advanced white belts may practice the prearranged movements called forms or "hyung" which they have learned. The intermediate students practice the forms for their level or perhaps the various combinations of movements used in free fighting. The advanced belts will execute the more complex forms of free fighting combinations.

The final part of the class often consists of free fighting. This is where two students compete against each other freely without prearrangement, putting to use the basic movements and combinations they have learned. Free fighting is restricted to advanced yellow belts and higher ranks.

At the end of the class, the students often kneel

down and close their eyes for a few minutes to allow their minds and bodies to recover from the strenuous movements they have been performing. The class closes the same way it began, with the ceremonial bow between the instructor and the students.

CLASS DISCIPLINE

The philosophy of the Oriental martial arts is based on respect, and this is what makes these arts distinctive from other physical sports. The Oriental philosophy of "respect the Elder and love the Younger" applies to all parts of life; children respect their parents, school students respect their teachers, martial arts trainees and followers respect their masters, and the citizens respect and obey the supreme ruler of a nation. Class discipline may be gradually developed through intensive training of offensive and defensive moves with due respect extended toward both fellow trainees and instructors, and thereby toward the arts.

Respect is not only for ability but also for seniority and rank, and trainees thus learn the meaning of "obedience." They learn to obey, to do what they are supposed to do and not do what they are not supposed to do. They learn an attitude of seriousness and patience which enables them to perfect techniques that are essential for improvement. When every trainee has the same attitude, the entire school becomes unified through discipline. Trainees with respect distinguish the martial arts gymnasium from the playground, and behave seriously during the class. They always bow with sincerity whenever they enter or leave the gymnasium. They address others with proper language and respect, and they understand that they are engaged in fighting arts which

must be practiced only under the limitations of proper rules and regulations.

Discipline becomes the outward sign of the inward mental control that trainees acquire. This mental control enables them to physically control their bodies and thus improve their techniques. Also, mental control accompanies the trainee out of the training gymnasium and enables him to perform better in all the aspects of his life. One cannot claim to be a true tae-kwon do man without discipline.

THE BOW

In oriental countries, the bow is used in martial arts as a sign of courtesy and respect especially for seniors in rank and instructors. The bow is returned by the seniors as a sign of their equal respect for the juniors.

The bow is performed by the trainees as a group to their instructor at the beginning and end of the class as explained in the section on the tae-kwon do class. Depending upon how the bow is made, it can be given several different meanings; obedience, sincerity and respect, friendliness, and martial arts type.

Several different types are shown in the photos.

THE KEE-UP

The kee-up is a single syllable sound which accompanies the expulsion of air from the lungs as a technique is performed with full strength. Avoid the beginner's common mistake of saying "kee-up" or "kiyai" when using it. You would not say "kee-up" any more than you would say "shout" when shouting.

In tae-kwon do, the kee-up has at least three purposes. First, the sudden expulsion of air from the lungs enables you to exert more force and tense your muscles. Second, the shout helps you to overcome any fear of your own when you face an opponent and, third, the loud noise frightens your opponent, momentarily giving you an opening.

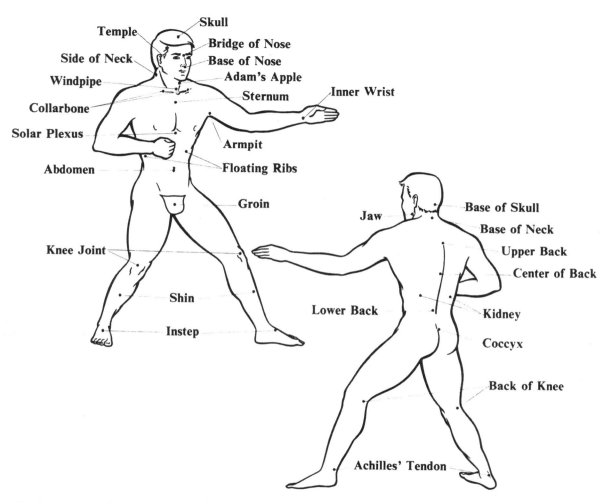

Temple
Skull
Bridge of Nose
Side of Neck
Base of Nose
Windpipe
Adam's Apple
Sternum
Inner Wrist
Collarbone
Solar Plexus
Armpit
Abdomen
Floating Ribs
Groin
Jaw
Base of Skull
Base of Neck
Upper Back
Center of Back
Knee Joint
Lower Back
Kidney
Shin
Coccyx
Instep
Back of Knee
Achilles' Tendon

Vital Spots of Human Body

CALISTHENICS

Calisthenics are an important part of the body conditioning necessary for the practice of tae-kwon do. There are two main types of calisthenics. There are first those which are performed for the purpose of loosening and limbering up the various parts of the body. The second are those like the push-up and sit-up, which are intended to strengthen the body.

Left: Slowly bend your neck so your head inclines forward as far as possible, then tilt your head back as far as you can. Center: Turn your head as far as possible to first one side and then the other. Right: Tilt your head to one side and then to the other.

Keeping your knees straight, bend over and try to touch the floor, then bend backward as far as you can.

Without leaning forward, stretch as far as possible to first one side and then the other.

With the knees straight, alternately try to touch the left toes with the right hand and the right toes with the left hand.

Slowly describe a circle with the upper part of your body in first one direction and then the opposite way so that you twist the trunk of the body.

With the supporting foot flat on the floor, lift the knee as high as possible toward your chest.

23

Keeping the knees straight, practice sit-ups as a good exercise for strengthening the stomach muscles.
The push-up shown here is performed on the knuckles. Beginners should not try to do too many push-ups on their knuckles, but instead should start with a few and gradually increase.

Stretch the leg from a front-facing position and also from the side.

24

One trainee hoists the other on his back and slowly bounces him up and down. The trainee being supported should always keep his body as limp as possible.

These are stretching exercise for the muscles of the back and sides of the thighs. The trainee performing the exercise should always keep his supporting foot flat on the floor.

First extend your left foot to the left side to a distance of about twice the width of your shoulders. Both knees must be bent equally and they must be slightly flexed outward to the sides, with both feet flat on the floor. Hips are pulled slightly backward as if you were sitting on the back of a horse. The upper part of the body is straight, with the chest open, stomach tightened and chin up. The upper body is in the center between the two legs. For a fist punch, bring the left fist to the waistline first and then punch as soon as you get into the stance.

HORSEBACK-RIDING STANCE (KEE-MAH SEH)

The horseback-riding stance, when you assume your opponent is on your side, is called a "side stance." You can move to your right side by first bringing your left foot to your right foot and then extending your right foot to the right. Or you cross your left foot behind your right foot (as shown in middle photo above) and extend right foot to the right. Finally, you can cross left foot over right foot and then extend right foot to the right. While stepping, you can practice making blocks, punches, strikes and side kicks.

The horseback-riding stance is the first tae-kwon do basic move that the beginners are taught in their first class. Punching exercises in the horseback-riding stance are usually performed at the beginning and end of the class. The practice of this stance gives trainees the good balance that is essential to tae-kwon do.

FORWARD STANCE (CHUN-GOOL SEH)

The forward stance is made by stepping back with your right foot. Your front knee must be bent and the lower part of the leg is straight. The toes of your front foot point straight forward. The back knee is locked, with the toes pointing outward at a forty-five degree angle. The distance between the front and rear foot is about twice the width of your shoulders, and you maintain a shoulder's width between the left and right foot so that the front part of your body can face straight forward. Sink your hips down by pressing the rear hip forward and downward. The upper part of the body stays straight, with the chin up and eyes looking forward. In the forward stance, you have about 60 percent of your body weight on your front foot.

The forward stance is the one most widely used in practicing basic moves such as blocks, punches, strikes and kicks. You must first practice the forward stance by just stepping forward and backward until the movements become natural to you. Then, combine the basic moves with the stance. The forward stance provides balanced position as well as an advancing force in basic drill.

27

Left: Bring your right foot forward next to the front foot in a natural way. Note that both knees are slightly bent and the upper part of the body is straight. Right: Bring the foot forward and outward at about a thirty-degree angle to the right, by first pushing forward with your rear hip. The entire step must be made in a single motion. You are now in a new forward stance which must be identical to the previous one. The advancing motion of your body is achieved through the speedy transfer of the body weight forward. This is assisted by the snapping motion of pushing your rear hip forward and the knee locking.

BACK STANCE (HOO-GOOL SEH)

The back stance is also made by stepping back on the right foot. The distance between the front and rear foot is about one and a half shoulder widths. Both feet stay flat on the floor and the heels are on a straight line facing toward the opponent. The toes of the front foot point straight forward and those of the rear to the right. Both knees are bent, with more weight on the rear leg, which is achieved by moving the front leg slightly toward the body and dropping the hips and bending the rear knee. As a result, your rear foot, hip and shoulder are on an almost vertical line. The upper part of the body stays upright but faces about forty-five degrees to the right. You look forward.

Stepping in back stance is somewhat easier than in forward stance. While stepping forward, keep both knees bent. When the steps are completed, hold the weight of the body on the rear leg, without transferring it forward as in the forward stance. Do not push your rear hip forward or downward. When you step backward, simply push your weight backward, holding it on the rear leg.

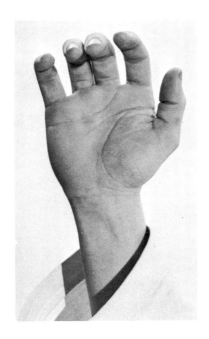

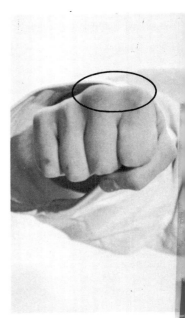

HOW TO MAKE A FIST

It is very important that you have a strong fist when you attempt to make punches and blocks. The fist should be firmly clenched and the wrist must be tightened. This way, your fingers, thumbs and wrist will not be hurt when a strong punch is landed on a real target.

Start with your hand open.

Bend the joints of the fingers inward. Curl the fingers into the palm. Squeeze them as tightly as you can so that the striking part of the hand is flat and square as shown in circle above.

Fold the thumbs inward over the fingers. When you punch, strike mainly with the first two knuckles.

A STRAIGHT FIST PUNCH

A straight fist punch with your right hand and your right leg forward in a forward stance, for example, is a forward punch. In order to practice a forward punch while stepping forward, make an exchange of the punch by thrusting the right fist forward, at the same time bring the left fist back to the cocked position as the step is completed. Make sure that the right shoulder remains straight and does not thrust forward.

To make a punch with your left fist at this moment, repeat the same procedure. While the left fist is thrusting forward, the right is simultaneously pulled back to a cocked position on the right side. Repeat the same procedure throughout the punching exercise.

As a beginner, you may complete stepping first and then execute your punch. To practice the forward punch while stepping backward, just reverse the procedure.

1– Cock your right fist on your right side, right over the belt line. Your right shoulder is closed and the fist is touching the body. 2– Begin to thrust the fist forward toward the imaginary target with the pushing motion of your right side. The left fist also begins to retreat to the left side for a reaction force for the punch.

3– When the fist is about halfway to the imaginary target, start to twist the wrist inward. 4– The fist is twisted with the palm facing downward. The wrist should be straight and tight. The left fist is cocked on the left for its turn. The upper part of your body stays upright and faces straight forward.

PRACTICE OF A REVERSE PUNCH

A straight fist punch with your left hand while your right leg is forward in a forward stance is a reverse punch. The execution of a reverse punch is often accompanied by a body twist which augments the punching force.

Left: Assume you are in a forward stance with right leg forward. You have just completed a reverse punch with left fist. Center: To make a reverse punch with your right fist, step forward with left side leaning slightly forward. Right hip is held slightly back. Right: As soon as step is completed, thrust right fist punch forward. Execution of the punch is aided by pushing motion of the right side forward and, at the same time, pushing motion of the hip downward.

KNIFE-HAND STRIKE (SHOOTO CHIGI)

Knife-Hand Edge—First, open your palm but press the fingers tightly together. The thumb is tucked down and also pressed back. Curl the fingers inward by slightly bending the first and second joints. Never bend the third joints. The striking edge is the area marked in the photo below. Remember that you must tighten the hand; otherwise, the hand will be injured when you strike a hard target.

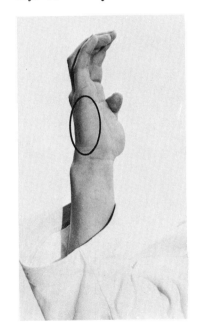

Outward Strike

Cock the right hand by placing it over the left shoulder, near the ear. The palm faces the cheek. Your body rotates slightly to face the left. Swing the hand in a forward-outward arc. At the same time, your body rotates back so the front part of the body faces straight forward. Your hand turns while striking so the palm faces downward at the impact. Make it a habit never to lock your elbow while striking. You may strike many spots with shooto, such as head, face, neck, collarbone and kidneys.

Inward Strike

Cock your right hand by raising it over the right shoulder near the ear. Your shoulder is open, and the elbow which is tightly bent presses backward.

Swing the hand in an inward arc so it strikes from an outside direction. At the impact of the strike, the palm faces upward. The hand is stopped at the center line of the body, with the elbow unlocked. The striking targets are about the same as those for the outward strike.

Downward Strike

Cock your right hand in the same manner as with the inward strike.

Execute the strike by bringing the elbow slightly forward first so that the hand swings in a downward arc. Strike in a vertical direction either by bringing the hand directly downward over the top of the head or shoulder, or in a descending curve on the collarbone. At the impact of the strike, the elbow is slightly bent.

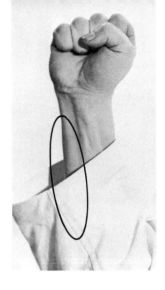   

LOW BLOCK (HAH-DAN MAKGI)

The low block is designed to block the opponent's kicks and punches which are aimed at the lower part of your body. The block is made by striking with the outer edge of your arm. When the block is executed in an outward direction, it is called an "outward low block." When it is made in a downward direction, it is called a "downward low block."

Outward Low Block—An outward low block is made first by raising your right arm in front of your left shoulder, with the palm several inches away from it. The palm faces your left cheek. You must always tighten your fist and arm. Then, swing the arm outward to your right side while straightening your elbow, which nonetheless always remains very slightly bent. While blocking, twist the arm inward so that the palm faces inward. Then, stop the arm directly over your right thigh. The distance between the fist and the thigh is about two fist lengths. Keep your chest widely open. Your left fist is pulled to the left waistline.

In order to practice an outward low block while stepping in forward stance, follow the photos and their captions:

← ⎯⎯⎯⎯⎯⎯⎯

While you begin the step, raise your right arm to block. Your body is slightly twisted toward the left side when the arm is raised. Notice that both knees are bent.

Execute the block as the step is completed. Twist the body back toward the right along with the block so that the front part of the body faces straight forward when the block is completed. The upper part of the body is upright. Note that you use both arms while executing the block. This gives the block more power, because the other arm provides a reaction force.

Downward Low Block

Raise your right arm to the left cheek with the fist tight. The palm faces the cheek. Swing the arm downward and, at the same time, outward until it reaches about two fist lengths over the right thigh. The arm is gradually twisted so that the palm faces inside when the block is completed. The elbow is very slightly bent. The left fist and shoulder are usually pulled backward when the block is delivered. This provides a thrusting motion for the movement of the right arm. The upper part of your body faces approximately forty-five degrees to the left. Look straight forward.

MIDDLE BLOCK (CHUNG-DAN MAKGI)

There are two basic ways of making the middle block—outward middle block and inward middle block.

Outward Middle Block—in order to make an outward middle block, first bring your right arm across the body, placing the fist near the left waist. The palm faces your body. Your body is slightly twisted toward the left side. While making the block, the body will twist back to a forward position. Swing the arm to the right slightly, twisting the arm outward. Stop the fist and elbow in front of your right side body line. The palm now faces upward. Your shoulder is slightly open, the elbow is bent and the fist remains parallel to the top of your shoulder. The block is made by striking with the inner surface of the arm.

Left: An outward middle block is often practiced in forward stepping. Center: While stepping, bring your right arm to the left ready to block. Your body is slightly twisted toward the left, with both knees bent.

Right: The outward middle block is executed as the step is completed. Note that while blocking, your body is tightened, the rear knee is locked, and the hip is pushed forward.

Inward Middle Block—The inward middle block is made by swinging your arm inward across the front part of the body. The striking surface is the outer edge of your arm.

In order to make an inward middle block, hold your right arm outside the right side body line. Your right shoulder is open, the fist stays slightly higher than shoulder height and the palm faces forward. You may bring your left arm across the front part of the body for a reaction force when executing the block. Then, swing the arm inward, across the body toward the solar plexus. The elbow, which is bent, stops in front of your solar plexus, several inches distant. The shoulder is closed. While blocking, the left fist comes all the way back to the left waistline for a reaction force.

The practice of an inward middle block in forward stepping is identical to that of an outward middle block, as shown in the photos.

HIGH BLOCK (SAHNG-DAN MAKGI)

The high block is used to protect the neck, face and head. There are three types of high blocks— the outward high block, the inward high block and the rising block. The outward high block is made in a similar manner to the outward middle block, except it is made for a high target area. There is also the same relationship between the inward high block and the inward middle block. The blocking areas are circled in photos below.

Outward high block.

Inward high block.

Rising Block (Chookyu Makgi)

Bring the right arm to the left across the front part of the body. The palm faces the body. The body is slightly twisted toward the left. Your left arm can also be placed across the body for a reaction force when the block is made.

Begin to raise your arm, twisting it forward. As soon as the arm passes your chest height, snap it up by forcing the elbow up and twisting it forward. At the same time, pull the arm slightly above your forehead, about two fists' distance away. The fist, with its palm facing forward, is slightly higher than the elbow.

LIMBERING-UP KICKS (BAHL OHLLIGI)

The purpose of limbering-up kicks is to gradually stretch the muscles under the legs and loosen the joints so that you can execute snap or thrust kicks effectively. After limbering up for months, you should be able to kick effectively. You can reach higher and focus better because you become less stiff through the limbering-up exercises. You are advised to exercise with limbering-up kicks continuously as long as you practice tae-kwon do.

Front Way
Bring your rear foot forward in order to raise all the way up. Flex the ankle back, at the same time, curling the toes. Your supporting knee must be slightly bent. Raise the kicking foot toward your body. The upper part of your body stays up-right to avoid falling. Then, bring the kicking foot back to the original position.

Side Way—Usually, the leg muscles are not loosened up in the beginning enough to deliver effective kicks to the side. Many months of continuous exercise will enable the students to lift their legs high enough to execute such kicks as side thrust and snap kicks and roundhouse kicks. Therefore, the limbering-up kick to the side or back becomes a special challenge to many tae-kwon do beginners.

In order to make a side limbering-up kick, swing the kicking foot up on your side with its heel portion slightly higher, while slightly bending the supporting knee. Watch the kicking foot from the right side while kicking. Avoid leaning downward too much while kicking.

43

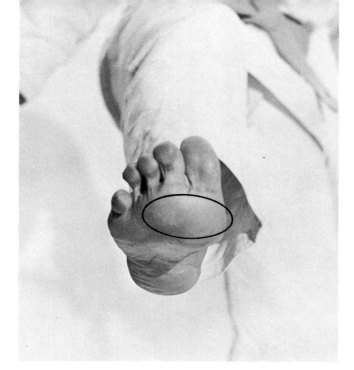

1, 2— To make a front kick with the rear leg in forward stance, first raise the knee and curl the toes upward. Be sure to keep the supporting foot flat on the floor throughout the move.

1

FRONT KICK (AHP CHAGI)

The front kick uses the ball of the foot to attack a variety of targets—usually the knee, groin, solar plexus and chin. It can be performed either with a snapping motion of the knee or with a thrusting motion of the hips. In the first case, the kick is very fast but lacks finishing power.

3– Kick out with either a snapping or thrusting motion as explained above. As soon as the kick is completed, bring your leg back to the raised knee position in order to maintain your balance.

4– You may either bring your kicking leg down in front of the supporting leg as shown in the photograph, or you may return it to the original position.

SIDE KICK (YUP CHAGI)

The outer edge of the foot is the striking surface for the side kick. Consequently the ankle must be flexed toward the inside of the leg. The targets for the side kick are usually the knee, solar plexus, ribs and face. Like the front kick, the side kick can be performed in either a snapping or thrusting motion.

From side stance, to make a kick with the right leg, step with the left leg going in front of the right.

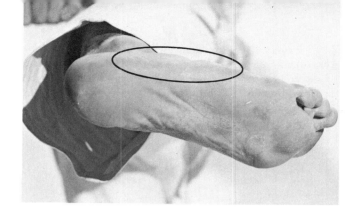

Raise the right leg with the knee toward the chest and the foot pointing outward.

Kick out with either a snapping or thrusting motion. Be sure to bring the leg back to its raised starting position before returning it to the floor.

RISING-HEEL KICK
(YUP DUIRO CHAGI)

This kick is somewhat similar to the side kick. The basic difference is that in the rising-heel kick the back of your hip faces the target, and consequently the direction of the kick is more to the back than to the side. The striking surface is the heel rather than the edge of the foot.

Look over your shoulder toward the target and, with the back of your hip facing the target, raise your knee.

Opposite: Kick out with the leg, going to the target in a rising motion. As with the other kicks, bring the kicking leg back to its raised position as soon as the kick is completed.

ROUNDHOUSE KICK
(TOHLLYU CHAGI)

The roundhouse kick is performed with a swinging motion of the hips and a snapping motion of the knee. The striking surface is the ball of the foot.

From forward stance, lift the kicking leg so the inside of the leg is parallel with the floor.

With a swinging motion of the hips and a snap of the knee, kick toward the target.

Bring the leg back to the body to maintain your balance before returning to the floor.

51

TAE KUK HYUNG (FORM)

Many forms or, in tae-kwon do terminology, "hyung" are practiced, going from fairly simple ones for beginners like Tae Kuk Hyung to the highly complex ones for advanced practitioners. Basically, they all consist of various offensive and defensive movements performed in sequence. The forms are intended to help the trainee develop speed, strength, accuracy and balance. To accomplish these objectives, the trainee must practice them constantly.

There are three Tae Kuk Hyung—Tae Kuk Cho

1— Starting position for Tae Kuk Hyung.
2— Step to the left in forward stance and perform low block. (#2—rising block, #3—outward middle block in back stance.)

3— Step forward with the right foot and execute middle target punch.
4— Turning through the right side on the right foot, make a low block in the opposite direction. (#2—rising block, #3—outward middle block in back stance.)

Dan (#1), Tae Kuk Yee Dan (#2) and Tae Kuk Sam Dan (#3). The steps and turns are the same in all three, but some of the stances and hand movements vary. The following photos illustrate Tae Kuk Cho Dan, which consists of the forward stance, low block, and straight middle target punch. The material in parentheses refers to those movements in Tae Kuk #2 and #3 which are different from #1. It is important that the steps be performed smoothly and the punches and blocks be executed with power and accuracy.

5— Step forward on the left foot and make a middle target punch.

6— Moving the left foot a half turn through the left side, perform a low block.

7— Stepping forward three times, execute three middle target punches with the right, left and right hands.

On the last punch, make a "kee-up." (#2—three spearhand thrusts, #3—three high target punches.)

8— Turn through your rear, moving the left foot to the right, and execute a low block. You are now at a right angle to your previous position. (#2—rising block, #3—outward middle block in back stance.)

5

6

7

8

53

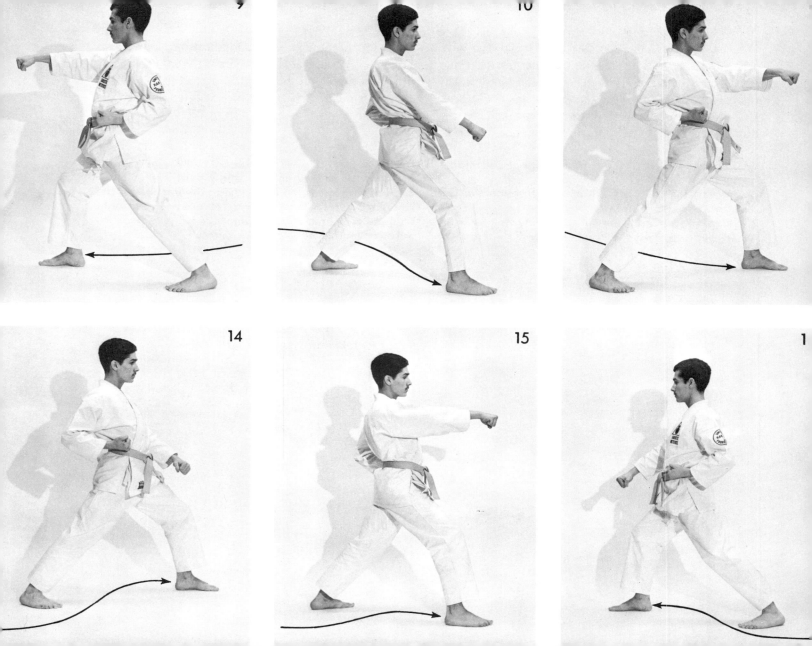

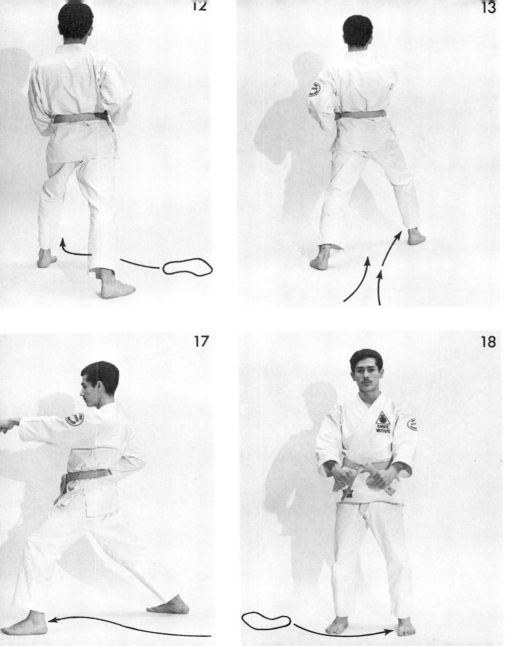

9– Step forward on your right foot with a middle target punch.

10– Turning on your right side with the right foot, execute a low block in the opposite direction. (#2—rising block, #3—outward middle block in back stance.)

11– Step forward on left foot, perform a middle target punch.

12– Moving the left foot a half turn through the left side, perform a low block.

13– Step forward three times, execute three middle target punches with the right, left and right hands. On the last punch, make a "kee-up." (#2—three low target punches, #3—three high target punches.)

14– Turn through your rear, moving the left foot to the right, and execute a low block. (#2—rising block, #3—outward middle block in back stance.)

15– Step forward on right foot and make a middle target punch.

16– Turning on your right side with the right foot, execute a low block in the opposite direction. (#2—rising block, #3—outward middle block in back stance.)

17– Step forward on left foot, perform a middle target punch.

18– Turning on your left side with the left foot, come back to your original starting position.

COMBAT COMBINATION #3

The combat combinations are similar to the forms in that they are a series of offensive and defensive movements performed in sequence. However, the combat combinations are performed at a faster speed than the forms. These combinations are more directly related to the moves used in free fighting than is the case with the forms. The constant practice of combat combinations should help the trainee apply a variety of offensive and defensive moves in free fighting.

The following combination is the third one that tae-kwon do trainees learn. Punches, blocks and kicks are practiced primarily in back stance in this combination.

1– The starting position is back stance low block position, with the left foot leading.

1

2– Execute a front kick with the right leg.

2

3— Come down to a back stance with the right leg leading. Simultaneously execute an outward middle block with the right hand.

4— Without stepping forward, execute a front kick with the right leg.

5— Stepping forward in back stance **on the left foot, per-**
form a middle target punch with the left hand. Then,
follow through with a reverse middle target punch
with the right hand.

6, 7— Bring the left leg up (without stepping) and execute a side kick.

8— Bring the kicking foot back to your body and step down into a side stance.

9— Turning to the front, perform a front kick with the right leg.

10— Come down to back stance with the right leg forward and execute a low block.

GLOSSARY

AHP CHAGI—Front Kick. A kick executed in forward direction.

BAHL OHLLIGI—Limbering-up kick. A kicking exercise mainly to loosen the leg muscles and joints.

BLACK BELT—Expert.

BROWN BELT—Fourth promotion and highest kup (First & Second Kup).

CHOOKYU MAKGI—Rising Block. An arm block executed in an upward direction to protect face area.

CHUNG-DAN MAKGI—Middle Block. An arm block to protect the mid-section of the body.

CHUN-GOOL SEH—Forward Stance. A basic stance, with slightly more weight on the front leg.

DAN—Black Belt Rank.

DO POK—Martial Arts Uniform.

GREEN BELT—Second promotion (Fifth & Sixth Kup).

HAH-DAN MAKGI—Low Block. An arm block executed downward mainly to protect the lower section of the body.

HOO-GOOL SEH—Back Stance. In this stance, both knees are bent, with slightly more weight on the rear leg.

HYUNG—Form. A series of basic techniques performed in a set pattern.

KEE-MAH SEH—Horseback-riding Stance. A basic stance in which the body weight is evenly distributed between the two legs.

KEE-UP—Shout. A single syllable sound which accompanies the expulsion of air from the lungs.

KUNG FU—Chinese Karate (or Martial Arts).

KUP—Rank lower than Black Belt.

KYOSA NIM—Instructor.

PURPLE BELT—Third promotion (Third & Fourth Kup).

SAHBUM NIM—Master.

SAHNG-DAN MAKGI—High Block. An arm block to protect the upper section of the body.

SHOOTO CHIGI—Knife-hand Strike. A strike with the side edge of a hand.

TAE KUK CHO DAN—Tae Kuk Form #1.

TAE KUK HYUNG—Tae Kuk Form. The basic forms for beginners.

TAE KUK SAM DAN—Tae Kuk Form #3.

TAE KUK YEE DAN—Tae Kuk Form #2.

TAE-KWON DO—Korean Karate.

TAE KYUN—Korean Karate. The name formerly used by Koreans.

TOHLLYU CHAGI—Roundhouse Kick. A kick delivered in an arc, from side to front.

WHITE BELT—Beginner.

YELLOW BELT—First promotion (Seventh & Eighth Kup).

YUP CHAGI—Side Kick. A kick executed to the side, hitting with the outer-edge of the foot.

YUP DUIRO CHAGI—Rising-Heel Kick. In this kick, striking surface is the heel of the foot.